For Girls!

Best Friends

Deborah Chancellor

QEB Publishing

Editor: Mandy Archer
Designer: Nikki Kenwood
Illustrator: Jessica Secheret

Published in the United States by
QEB Publishing, Inc.
3 Wrigley, Suite A
Irvine, CA 92618

www.qed-publishing.co.uk

be

or

Library of Congress Cataloging-in-Publication Data

Chancellor, Deborah.
 Best friends / Deborah Chancellor.
    p. cm. -- (For girls!)
 Includes index.
 Summary: "This guide for girls gives advice on things to do with
best friends, including sleepovers, parties, secrets and dares, texts and
blogs, and friendship gifts"--Provided by publisher.
 ISBN 978-1-60992-105-7 (library binding)
 1. Best friends--Juvenile literature. 2. Female friendship--Juvenile
literature. 3. Amusements--Juvenile literature. I. Title. II. Series.

 BF575.F66C43 2012
 646.70083'42--dc22

                        2011006914

ISBN 978 1 60992 105 7

Printed in China

Picture credits
(t=top, b=bottom, l=left, r=right, c=center, fc=front cover)
Getty Images 5t Steve Gorton and Karl Shone; **iStockphoto** 5l kickers; **Photolibrary** 8b Leanne Temme, 11t
Ester Sorri; **Rex** 18l Image Source/Rex Features,19r Burger/Phanie/Rex Features, 21tr Image Source/Rex Features,
21lc Design Pics Inc/Rex Features, 28r OJO Images/Rex Features; **Shutterstock** 4b wavebreakmedia ltd, 4
blue67design and azzzya (spot art), 6r R. Gino Santa Maria (girl on right), 6r Andresr (girl on left), 6b Christiana
Mustion, 7b laola, 7b Bukhavets Mikhail (spot art), 9 Callahan (spot art), 9b Pinkcandy, 11c Elena Schweitzer, 12b
Sparkling Moments Photography, 13b linnik, 14l ArrowStudio, LLC, 14b Dmitry Kolmakov, Coprid, Nika Novak,
15t a9photo, 15 Roslen Mack (spot art), 15l Zand,
16 Lavanda and nata_danilenko (spot art),16r LittleRambo, 17l Ruth Black, 17c Mike Flippo, 17b Lev Dolgachov,
18r c.byatt-norman, 19t sandra zuerlein and 1000 Words Images, 19 Elise Gravel (spot art), 20c liskus, 22b Fesus
Robert, 23bl Huntstock.com, 23br stoyanh, 24l ArrowStudio, LLC, 25b Monkey Business Images, 26 PILart (spot
art), 26b NinaMalyna, 27t clickthis (spot art), 27t saras66, 27tr Duncan de Young, 27r tatniz, 27c Alena Rozova,
27b Cre8tive Images, 29t Anke van Wyk.

Be web wise! Neither the publishers not the author can be responsible for the content of any
websites that you visit or any third-party websites. Always check with an adult before going
online and ask their permission before registering any details on a new site.

Contents

Friends Forever!

A best friend is a person to treasure. A true BFF (Best Friend Forever) is there to share the good times and the bad, ready to stand by you no matter what. Where would you be without your best friend?

Sharing Secrets

Best friends will listen to your secret hopes and dreams, as well as your worries. You must be able to trust your best friend not to tell a soul, and your best friend has to trust you, too!

Keeping in Touch

Friends love to talk all the time! There are lots of ways to keep in touch. Swap phone numbers or instant message a smiley face to your friend's PC. Texting is often cheaper than talking by phone—and just as much fun.

:) HAPPY
:(SAD
:O SHOCKED
:S CONFUSED
;) WINK
:D LAUGHING

Special Tokens

Exchange a gift with your best friend to show how much you care. You could even buy a special necklace with two matching halves. Keep one half each, so that every time you look at it you think of your best friend.

Friendship Bracelets

Learn how to weave friendship bracelets using knotted lengths of embroidery yarn. Surprise your best friend by giving her a friendship bracelet made with her favorite colors.

Old Friends

Having a new best friend can be so exciting, it's easy to forget about the rest of your buddies. Try not to make your old friends feel left out—introduce them to your BFF and invite them on playdates.

New Friends

Just because you have a best friend, it doesn't mean you can't make new friends, too! If your best friend doesn't like this, tell her how special she is and ask her to join in. Soon, you'll all be friends together!

School's Cool

School can be a lot of fun—it's the perfect place to make friends and get to know them better. Work hard, but make the most of your recess, too.

Who's the New Girl?

If a new girl arrives in your class, make an effort to talk to her. She is probably nervous and a bit shy. Introduce her to your friends and invite her to play with you at recess.

Crazy Crazes

What's the latest collecting craze at school? Perhaps it is stickers, key chains or gel pens. If your teacher won't allow you to bring collections into the playground, arrange trades with your friends at home.

Fun things to collect:
- magazines
- postcards
- buttons
- key chains
- gel pens
- stickers
- beads
- bookmarks
- barretts

Miss You!

It can be tough if someone you like moves away or changes school. Take the plunge and try to make some new friendships. You can always keep in touch with your old friend, and she wouldn't want you missing her or feeling

Playground Games

Long recesses will flash by if you round up your buddies for some playground games. Have you tried making up clapping rhymes that get faster and faster? Ask your teacher for some new ideas, or for help in agreeing the rules.

Beat the Bullies

If a person at school keeps saying and doing hurtful things to you, it can be very upsetting. If you think you are being bullied, talk to an adult you trust and they will help fix the problem.

Time for Tact

If you're taking a day trip or having a special meal and can only invite a few friends, don't hand out the invitations in front of everyone at school. It's a kind way of making sure the girls you can't invite don't feel left out.

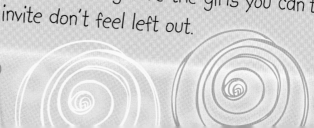

Samantha

Please come to my birthday party at Grove House, on Saturday at 6 o'clock.

Lots of love

Rachel xxxxx

Who Likes Who?

Everyone wants to be popular, with friends lining up for their attention! It can be easy to forget that quality is more important than quantity.

Little Miss Popular

Some girls like being part of a big gang, while others are happy to hang out with one or two close friends. Both are good choices— we are all different, so different things make each of us happy.

Look out for Each Other

To have a good friend you need to be a good friend. Take time to talk to your friend if she is upset and listen to her problems. Stick up for her and never make her worries seem silly.

Top Topics for Starting Friendships

Favorite movies, bands, books, clothes, school classes, candies.

Make the First Move

The best way to make friends is to be friendly! When you meet someone new, tell them your name and ask what they are called. Invite them to join in your game and chat while you play.

Kindness Counts

If you want your friends to like you, be thoughtful and don't say cruel things behind their back. Relax and be yourself and they are sure to want to spend time with you.

Be Yourself

You don't have to copy everything that your friends say and do. Listen to your heart and stay true to yourself. The best friends are the people who accept you as you are, not the ones who want to change you.

Good Friends...

listen as well as talk

defend you every time

never abandon a friend in need

always make you smile!

Fitting In

Do you ever feel under pressure to do something just because a friend told you to? If one of your pals is being bossy, find the courage to stand up to her. You might be surprised how many of your other friends are secretly feeling the same way!

Forgive and Forget

Arguments can erupt over the tiniest things! Don't let fights drag on—try to make up as soon as you can.

Three's a Crowd?

Sometimes it is tough for three friends to get along together. If two of you get super-close, the third person might feel left out. If this happens in your group of friends, talk about it. Things will get better if you explain how you feel.

Copycats

Friends sometimes argue because one thinks the other is copying them. Remember that if your friend copies you, it is really because she likes you. Take it as a compliment and enjoy setting the trend!

Gossip Girl

If one of your friends discovers that you have said unkind things about her, there's sure to be a bust-up. Before you fight back, take a moment to imagine how she must be feeling. Talk the problem over and you'll end up closer than before.

Say Sorry

After a fight, never be too proud to say sorry. Even if you didn't cause the argument, it's easy to say cruel things in the heat of the moment. If your friend apologizes to you, let her know that you forgive her.

Making Up is Fun to Do

Don't let an argument spoil a top friendship! Patch things up with a big hug, some kind words, and a sparkly smile. If you really want to show your friend you are sorry, you could even give her a little gift or write her a note.

Sorry

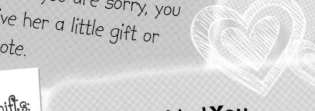

Super "I'm sorry" gifts:

cupcakes
nail polish
homemade jewelry
a picture or poem

Put it Behind You

Once you have made up with your friend, forget the argument ever happened. It is not fair to bring it up the next time that something goes wrong. Move on to the good times instead!

Party Time

A birthday is the perfect excuse to plan an unforgettable party for you and your friends.

Who's Coming?

First things first—find out how many people you can invite, then write a guest list. Try to pick pals who get along well together. If you leave out any of your best friends there could be trouble!

Choose a Theme

It's decision time. What kind of party do you want? If you love to dress up, choose a glam theme like "Disco Divas." If you'd prefer an active party, pick your favorite sport and ask your parents to make a reservation at the venue.

Design Time

Design your party invite on a laptop or PC. Choose a funky font for the words and paste in pictures to fit the theme. Don't forget to add all the vital information, such as the date, time, and place!

Setting the Scene

Homemade decorations make a party extra special. Try painting banners and decorating balloons. You could even use photos of your friends to make place cards, so they know where to sit at the party table.

Stand on your head for five seconds

Sing a pop song like an opera star

Giggles and Games

When your friends arrive, persuade them to try some fun party games. Limbo dancing and charades are great icebreakers, especially if you hand funny forfeits to your guests when they get caught out!

Party Playlist

You'll need music at your party, so make a playlist of your favorite songs on your MP3 player. Why not burn the playlist onto some CDs and give them as party favors for your friends to take home at the end?

Theme It!

Have you ever hosted a themed party? When your birthday comes around this year, try something a little different. Whether it's a beach grill, a costume disco, or a pampering afternoon—the choice is up to you!

Pop Stars

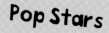

If you're always singing along to pop songs, throw a karaoke party. Get a karaoke DVD or computer game, then invite your friends to come dressed as pop stars. The most dazzling costume and performance get a prize!

Crafty Creations

If you and your friends love making things, collect some funky beads and craft materials for a jewelry-making party. At the end of the festivities your guests will be able to take their fabulous creations home.

Yummy pizza toppings

✿ olives and mozzarella
✿ chicken and mushroom
✿ pepperoni and chilli
✿ tuna and peppers

Pizza Parlor

Lay out some pizza bases and a selection of tasty toppings, then invite your friends to decorate their meal before they eat it. Your pals will be flocking to your pizza party quicker than you can say "Mamma mia!"

Hop, Flip, Jump!

Ask your parents if you can host a super-springy trampoline party. A coach at your local sports center will teach you and your friends some cool tricks, so you can all learn to bounce in style.

Skate Time

Roller- and ice-skating are fantastic fun! Invite your friends to a party in the park, or groove and glide at your nearest rink. Prepare for some tumbles before you get the hang of it! You might just discover a cool new hobby...

Strike!

Anyone can enjoy ten-pin bowling—beginners may discover a hidden talent and experienced bowlers can always improve their game. Split your friends into teams and let everyone choose a silly name. The team with the highest score could even get prizes!

Snacks and Treats

Getting ready for a party can be just as much fun as the celebration itself! Plan a few mouth-watering surprises and your big day is guaranteed to be a huge success.

Make Up a Menu

Decide what kind of party food will tickle your friends' tastebuds. Remember to organize some vegetarian options for anyone who doesn't eat meat. If one of your guests has a food allergy, check that your choices are safe for her to eat.

Make Up a Menu

cupcakes
chocolate-covered fruit
tacos
mini pizzas
sandwiches
mini donuts
cookies
popcorn

Celebration Cake

Choosing the party cake is the birthday girl's privilege! If the cake is baked at home, help decorate it to match your party theme. Will you choose a tower of pretty pink cupcakes or a delicious chocolate gateau?

Sweet Surprise

A chocolate fountain is a machine that melts chocolate for dipping at special occasions. Ask your parents to hire one for your birthday party, then take turns dipping in marshmallows, strawberries, and gingerbread shapes.

Party Piñata

A party piñata is a game and a treat all rolled into one! Buy or make one, then fill it with mini candies and gifts. Blindfold each other, then take turns to whack the piñata with a stick until the treats scatter onto the floor!

Going Home Time

At the end of your party, give your friends a pretty bag stuffed with gifts, balloons, and candy. Buy the bags in advance and put names on them so that nobody misses out. Don't forget to pop in a slice of party cake, too!

Essential Sleepover Kit

Checklist:
- ✓ PJs
- ✓ cell phone
- ✓ toothbrush
- ✓ snacks
- ✓ clean clothes
- ✓ games console
- ✓ DVDs
- ✓ flashlight
- ✓ slippers

So you're going to a sleepover—be prepared! You'll have even more fun if you remember to take all the right things with you.

Arrive in style

Make a good impression on your friends with a cool sleepover bag. Ask at home if you can have an old, small suitcase, then customize it with stickers and pictures of your favorite TV and pop stars.

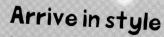

Making Memories

Bring a cell phone so you can take funny photos of your friends at the sleepover. Later on, you can also text home to say goodnight to your family.

Night, night!

18

Fun and Games

Don't forget to charge up your games console and pack it in your bag. If you have a favorite DVD, bring that along, too, so you can watch a midnight movie with your friends.

Midnight Munchies

No sleepover would be complete without a proper midnight feast. Spend your allowance on some sweet treats to share in the middle of the night. Don't expect to bring any candy home!

Home Comforts

Don't forget your toothbrush—you'll need to clean your teeth after all that candy! Bring your own comfy pillow to help you to fall asleep—if your friends give you the chance, that is...

Special Cuddles

Last, but not least, don't leave home without your bedtime stuffed animal. He'll be lonely staying behind without you, and if you start to feel homesick at the sleepover, he will make you feel a lot better.

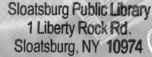

Sloatsburg Public Library
1 Liberty Rock Rd.
Sloatsburg, NY 10974

Giggle the Night Away

The last thing you'll want to do at your sleepover is get much sleep! It's fun to stay up late with your friends, and there are all sorts of games that you can play to keep awake.

Sooo Spooky!

Flick off the light then switch on a flashlight. Huddle together and see who can tell the scariest ghost story. Don't scream too loudly or you'll wake up the neighbors!

Wink Murder

Choose a friend to be a "detective" then send her out of the room. Decide who is to be the "murderer," then call the detective back in. The murderer "kills" her victims by winking at them, one by one. Can your detective catch the culprit in the act?

Truth or Dare?

When the rest of the household finally goes to bed, play this game with your friends. Flip a coin—if it's heads, tell a secret, and if it's tails, do something daring—like going downstairs in the dark all by yourself.

Get a nightmare makeover!

Switch clothes with the girl sitting next to you

Movie Marathon

Choose a bunch of movies starring your favorite actor, then watch them all back-to-back! Who can stay awake until the final closing credits? Make a "greatest fan" badge to present to the winner at breakfast-time!

Camping Out

In the summer, try hosting a camping sleepover. Put up a tent in your backyard, and ask your friends to bring flashlights, sleeping bags, and warm pajamas. Don't get spooked by all the nighttime noises!

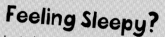

Feeling Sleepy?

Waking up the next morning won't be easy. Try not to doze off during the day, no matter how tired and grumpy you feel. Go to bed early the next night and you'll soon catch up on your missed beauty sleep!

21

Sharing and Switching

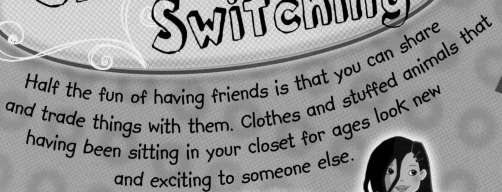

Half the fun of having friends is that you can share and trade things with them. Clothes and stuffed animals that having been sitting in your closet for ages look new and exciting to someone else.

Instant Makeover

If you are the same size as your friend, you could do a clothes trade. It doesn't have to be permanent— you could just borrow something for a week. Check that your mom or dad is happy with the idea first.

Cuddly Exchange

Ask your friends to bring over a stuffed animal that they don't want any more. Put them in a heap and take turns to choose a "new" toy to play with. Make a deal to meet in a month's time to have another switch around.

Trade Off

There's no limit to the things you can trade! What about exchanging DVDs, accessories, or magazines? It's best if you meet at a friend's house to do this and check at home before you give away anything valuable.

Try trading:
DVDs, jewelry, CDs, books, shoes, barretts, clothes, computer games

Give it Away

At Christmas or on your birthday, you may get two of the same gift. If this happens, don't sulk, but give your best friend the "double." Perhaps she'll share her gifts with you next time.

Yard Sale

Have a clear out in your bedroom and persuade your friends to do the same. Meet up with your stuff and agree one fixed price for every item on sale. Take a little bit of money and buy the things you fancy. Spend the profits on a group treat, or make a donation to charity.

Pamper Parlor

Ask your friends to bring some make-up round to your house, so you can share it and try out new looks. Don't forget to take some "before" and "after" photos for a laugh!

Chatting and Blogging

There are lots of ways to connect with friends online—just be sure to check first that it's OK with your mom or dad.

Online Games

There are so many games that you can play online. Before you start, text your friends to ask if they are free to play, too. You can even instant message while you play—just type something and wait for a reply!

Text Together

Texting is a great way to keep in touch. When you get a text, you know your friend is thinking about you! Always reply to your friend's texts or send her a smiley to show that you care.

Chatting Online

Social networking sites are really for teenagers and adults, but there are some special ones for preteens. Always ask before logging on to new sites and be very careful about who you chat to.

Get Blogging

A blog is an online journal, where you type your thoughts and people reply. If you'd like to set one up ask your mom or dad to help you. Always show them your blog entries before you publish online.

Txt Talk

2MORO	Tomorrow
CU L8R	See you later
EZ	Easy
GR8	Great
LOL	Laugh out loud
RUOK?	Are you OK?
THX	Thanks

Cyber Bullying

Chatting online is fun, but sometimes people can write messages that are unkind. This is called "cyber bullying." If anyone is nasty or rude to you online, tell your parents or a teacher so they can sort it out. Don't let the bully win.

Keep it safe online

- **Don't** arrange to meet anyone you have only chatted to on the Internet.
- **Don't** give away your real name, birthday, address, or phone number.
- **Don't** say where you go to school, or anything about your family.
- **Don't** post photos or information that could be used to hurt you or any of your friends.
- **Do** use strict security settings in chat rooms, so only friends you list can chat to you.

Rainy Day Ideas

Do you dread getting stuck indoors on a rainy day? Grab some friends, then give one of these boredom-busting ideas a try!

Terrific Tresses

Set up a hair salon in your bathroom and start creating new hairstyles for your friends. Try high ponytails, loose topknots, and eye-catching braids. Don't use scissors though—cutting is for the experts!

Pamper Yourselves!

Have a go at making luscious natural face packs. Try smearing on mashed avocado with a few drops of almond oil, or oatmeal mixed with natural yogurt. Soothe your eyes with slices of cool cucumber before you wash it all off!

Nail Bar

Tell your friends to bring their nail polish round to your place. Set up a nail station in the kitchen and paint each other's nails. Be creative—invent patterns, stick on gems, and use lots of glossy colors.

Old-fashioned fun

Computer games are great, but sometimes it's fun to switch off the PC and go back to basics. Dig out your old board games from the closet, think up some crazy new rules, then challenge your friends to a match.

Cookie flavors: chocolate chips, marshmallows, peanuts, cherries, coconut, lemon zest

Get Baking

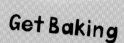

Find a good, easy recipe for cookies and combine the ingredients. Follow the instructions and get baking! Which flavors will you stir in? Ask an adult for help when using the oven.

Duck and Dive

If it's wet outside, go swimming! It's a fantastic way to have fun and keep fit. The more friends you swim with, the better—so cal them all up and arrange a time to meet at your local pool.

Out and About

The sun is shining, so don't sit around waiting for something exciting to happen! Grab your shades and head outside.

Check it Out

Always let your mom and dad know what your plans are. Agree a time to get back and wear your watch so that you won't be late. Take your cell phone and keep it switched on all the time.

Retail Therapy

Hit the shopping mall with a friend. Help each other to choose something stylish, like a bag, a necklace, or a funky hair accessory. Don't worry if you both want to buy the same thing— maybe you could pretend to be twins!

On Your Bike

If it's a long walk to your friends' place, cycle there, then go on a bike ride together. Check the route first at home to make sure it is safe—and don't forget to wear your bike helmet.

Secret Fort

Make a fort at the bottom of your backyard or ask your parents to take you to the park. Find a tree with low branches and hang an old blanket over them. Take cushions to sit on and snacks to eat inside your fort.

Other Fun Ways to Get About:
go-karts
roller blades
skateboards
scooters

Safe Spot

Always play in safe places with your friends. Never hang out near a railroad line or busy road. Stay away from construction sites and deserted spots. If you're not sure about a place, don't go and play there.

Stranger Danger

When you are out, remember the golden rule—never talk to strangers. Keep on walking even if the person is friendly and offers you gifts or candy. Never accept a ride from someone you don't know very well.

Best Friends' Quiz

What sort of best friend are you? Find a piece of paper, then write down the answers to this special friendship quiz.

1. What should you do to keep your best friend happy?
    a never make any new friends
    b ignore all your old friends
    c keep your best friend's secrets

2. What is the best way to make friends?
    a buy people gifts
    b talk and listen to people
    c wear the same clothes as everyone else

3. How do you make up after an argument?
    a say sorry and hug your friend
    b tell your friend she was wrong
    c never forget what happened

4. How do you decide on your party guest list?
    a invite everyone in your class, so you get lots of gifts
    b choose friends who get along well together
    c pick the most popular girls

5. How do you make sure your party food is a success?
    a choose all your favorite snacks and treats
    b leave all the decision-making to someone else
    c make sure there is a variety of food for everyone to enjoy

6. **What should you do if you take your favorite candy to a sleepover?**

   a eat your friends' candy and keep your own to take home

   b share them with all your friends

   c let your friends eat some, but save most for yourself

7. **How do you react if your friend texts you?**

   a ignore it

   b wait a few days then reply

   c reply as soon as you can

8. **Your friend asks you to give her a new hairstyle. What do you do?**

   a agree to the idea—if she does your hair afterward

   b cut her hair short

   c refuse to touch her hair

Look back at these pages: Friends Forever! (pages 4-5); Who Likes Who? (pages 8-9); Forgive and Forget (pages 10-11); Party Time (pages 12-13); Snacks and Treats (pages 16-17); Essential Sleepover Kit (pages 18-19); Chatting and Blogging (pages 24-25); Rainy Day Ideas (pages 26-27)

How Well Did You Do?

Count your correct answers below to find out!

0-3 You're on the right track, but there's lots more to learn about being a good friend and staying true to yourself.

4-6 Pretty good! You are great at meeting new people and being buddies with the friends that you've got.

7-8 You're the best! Most girls would love a friend like you— keep up the good work!

Quiz answers: 1. c, 2. b, 3. a, 4. b, 5. c, 6. b, 7. c, 8. a

Index